Wicked
QUICKIES

52 WAYS TO GET IT ON ANYTIME, ANYWHERE

AUDACIA RAY

SOURCEBOOKS CASABLANCA™
AN IMPRINT OF SOURCEBOOKS, INC.®
NAPERVILLE, ILLINOIS

Published by Sourcebooks Casablanca, an imprint of Sourcebooks, Inc.
P.O. Box 4410, Naperville, Illinois 60567-4410
(630) 961-3900
Fax: (630) 961-2168
www.sourcebooks.com

Library of Congress Cataloging-in-Publication Data

Ray, Audacia.
   Wicked quickies : 52 ways to get it on anytime, anywhere / by Audacia
Ray.
      p. cm.
   1. Sex instruction. 2. Sexual excitement. I. Title.
HQ56.R39 2009
613.9'6—dc22

                              2009025668

          Printed and bound in the United States of America.
              SP 10 9 8 7 6 5 4 3 2 1

CONTENTS

INTRODUCTION

The quickie.

At the most basic level, a quickie is a speedy sex act. And "speedy" plus "sex" often gives the impression that not everyone walks away happy.

But it doesn't have to be that way.

A hasty coupling can add a little jolt to your day, a little satisfaction on the go. *Wicked Quickies* is your guide to making the most of such fast and furious action. Packed with fifty-two ways to get it on anywhere, anytime, *Wicked Quickies* boasts an entire year's worth of spontaneous ecstasy. Flip to an entry once a week, let the erotic sketches inspire you, and read on for a brief description of the selected quickie along with sexy anecdotes and useful tips.

Now comes the best part: get down and dirty using each entry as inspiration. Because each suggested act has a risqué rating of one, two, or three (with one being somewhat tame and three being extra naughty and erotic), you can tailor the experience to your mood or personality.

Not one to play by the rules? Make up your own. Pick a page, but don't show it to your lover. Then surprise him with this mystery quickie when he least expects it! Or leave a copy of this book where you know she'll discover it and let her savor the anticipation all day long.

Note that the beauty of a quickie isn't always in reaching the finish line. Sprinkled throughout *Wicked Quickies* are entries focused on quick encounters that will leave you wanting more.

Whatever your pleasure, getting down and dirty in a hurry has never been more fun.

A note of caution: having sex in public places is sometimes against the law. Be aware of the attention your activities may cause!

Quick • ie

Pronunciation: *Kwik-ee*

Meaning: *Spontaneous sexual activity*

Function: *Instant gratification*

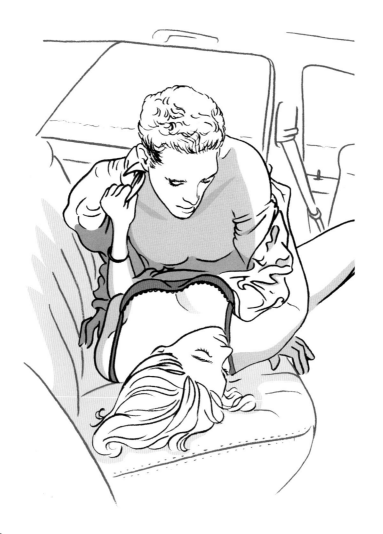

THE HUMP SEAT

Risqué Level ●●●

Maybe it's the heat, the speed, the feeling of freedom and escape, or just the naughtiness, but cars can make lovers feel extra frisky! Turn your own car into a road-going sex machine.

Pull over in a parking lot or the breakdown lane for a fast quickie while you're on the road, and re-create your teenage years. You know you'll enjoy the ride.

QUICKIE HOT TIP

Sitting positions are best suited for car sex, unless you have the option of spreading out in the back of your SUV or pickup. (See Quickie 41, Truckin'.)

SIT AND SPIN

Risqué Level ●○○

The washing machine's spin cycle is a great moment to take time out for a spin with your partner. Turn a mundane chore into a fun frolic—and turn an unsexy appliance into a giant vibrator. Quickies aren't really designed to encourage female orgasm, but a little mechanical nudge can go a long way toward achieving it. Even though the washing machine can't offer direct clitoral stimulation, ladies, it can help relax all kinds of muscles when you sit on it.

QUICKIE HOT TIP

Dial up the risk level if you dare. For level one, stick to your basement laundry room. For level two, test out an empty room in an apartment or condo building. Partner action in a Laundromat earns you a three.

A SHAVE AND A BJ

Risqué Level ●○○

Like many quickies, this one is best performed as a sneak attack. Wait until his focus is on the delicate act of shaving before dropping to your knees to take care of business. Guys, part of the fun is how careful you both have to be so you can survive the shave without any nicks, cuts, or early climaxes.

QUICKIE HOT TIP

If you have extra time and want to get a little carried away, decorate yourself. Ladies, create a full-on shaving-cream bikini to really send him over the edge. Before you know it, you both will be rinsing it off in a hot shower.

4

FELLATIO PHONE CALL

Risqué Level ●●○

Sorting out service issues with your phone, cable, or electric company is never fun, but a blow job can do wonders to make an irritating conversation with a customer service representative much more bearable. Why not reach out and touch someone?

"One of the little things I do for my wife is deal with the cable company, because they always seem to be messing something up. I was on a particularly long and irritating call when she came into the room with a seductive grin and got down on her knees in front of me. Good thing I was on hold most of the time—I wouldn't have been able to stop moaning even if there was a person on the other end of the line!"

–Peter, 38

10

EARLY BIRD SPECIAL

Risqué Level ●●○

Turn your usual after-work routine into a sexy surprise. On a day when you know he'll be working late, use the time to your advantage. Rush home, undress, and put on a sexy pair of panties and heels. Then strike a pose when you know he'll be walking through the door.

And guys, don't let working girls miss out on the fun. Strip off that shirt and slide on only a tie so her day at the office has a happy ending.

The rest should be quickie history.

QUICKIE HOT TIP

If you can't hear your partner's car in the driveway or footsteps in the hall, and don't want to stand in the foyer on watch, pull a chair into view of the front door, sit, and begin to play with yourself. You'll be comfy, raring to go, and ready to offer dessert before you've even had dinner!

BOX LUNCH

Risqué Level ● ● ○

Break up your humdrum workday by meeting your partner in an unexpected environment. A lunchtime quickie at a hotel where you have to inquire about the rate for a "short stay" will feel naughty enough to get your blood pumping and secretive enough that you'll have something to laugh about later. An afternoon delight is just as delicious and satisfying as that lunch you packed in the morning and didn't get a chance to eat.

QUICKIE HOT TIP

Write your lover a little note, and stick it in your partner's brown-bag lunch with instructions on when and where to meet, as well as what he or she should (or should not!) be wearing.

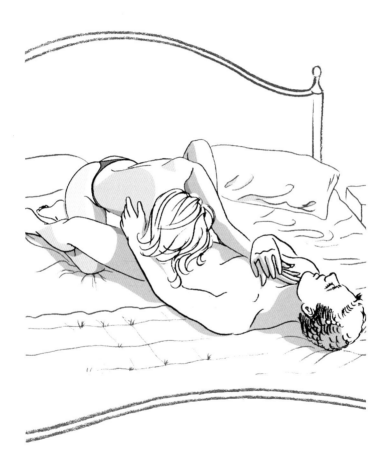

⋙ 7 ⋘

WAKE-UP CALL

Risqué Level ●○○

Just because he's asleep doesn't mean everything about him is. Ducking under the covers and wrapping your lips around his morning wood will have him wanting to rub more than just his sleepy eyes.

"My husband is seriously not a morning person. In fact, he's not even really a person until he's had that first cup of coffee. But I've found that a blow job is a million times better than coffee. Let's just say he considers it the breakfast of champions!"

–Jessica, 31

BACK ALLEY SHAG

Risqué Level ●●●

If you just can't wait to get home after a night out dancing, popping into a back alley for a quickie will make you feel both naughty and relieved. You can also turn this into cops-and-robbers role playing. Just practice saying, "Put your hands up against the wall and spread 'em," in your best sexy, threatening tone of voice.

QUICKIE HOT TIP

A tiny flashlight on your keychain will help you quickly survey the area for things like unappetizing garbage and broken glass. You wouldn't want your quickie to quickly become something you have to explain in an emergency room. This one works better if you're standing or leaning on something safe!

17

POWDER ROOM PETTING

Risqué Level ●●●

Sex and bar bathrooms go together like martinis and olives. When you have a few drinks in you and a hottie at your side, the urge to shake and stir sometimes cannot be resisted. Ladies, you can prop yourself up on the sink, and then you can both use the mirror for an added dimension to your pleasure.

QUICKIE ETIQUETTE

If you want to ensure that you have ample time to execute your quickie without alerting (or annoying!) all the other bar patrons, make sure the bar has more than one bathroom before you enact your horny takeover.

10

MANUAL TRANSMISSION

Risqué Level ●●○

Let your hands wander as you wander the road. You can spice up a long drive for her, using your fingers like windshield wipers to rub her clitoris back and forth. Turn him on by stroking his "stick shift," accelerating gradually, so he'll have time to build up his speed. These driving exercises will help to keep you limber and get each other warmed up for when you reach your final destination. Driving while distracted can be dangerous, of course—pull over if the moment gets to be too much.

> I love when my husband and I grope each other like horny teenagers in the car! There is something so hot about driving along, when no one else knows what you're doing, or why you're steaming up the windows. Plus, the fact that we can only go to second base makes our arrival home all the more exciting!"
>
> –Stacey, 34

THE (UN)DRESSING ROOM

Risqué Level ●●●

Women always like a second opinion when trying on potential wardrobe additions, so most ladies' dressing-room attendants won't bat an eye if you both disappear behind the curtains or locked doors. Pick a changing room at a distance from other shoppers, and put on your own private fashion show. If you hit the stores at odd hours, you'll be more likely to find deserted rooms just waiting for your erotic fashion show. Guys, don't be surprised if you soon overcome your dislike of shopping!

QUICKIE HOT TIP

Remember to be discreet, especially if the changing room walls don't reach the floor! If you can, pick a firm wall. Put your back against it while wrapping your legs around your partner's waist. It's tough to maintain this position for a long time, but it's certainly good for a quick thrill. And that's all you're after, right?

~ 12 ~

FERVENT FOOTSIE

Risqué Level ●●○

The beauty of a quickie isn't always in going "all the way." Sometimes it's just as fun to stay clothed and engage in a little stealthy naughtiness that will leave you both wanting more. Whether you're at the office, discussing stocks and bonds with your secret work paramour, or at a meeting with your partner about your real estate holdings, kick off a shoe and gently work your toes on his package underneath the table. The rest of the attendees will be none the wiser.

QUICKIE HOT TIP

Bare feet are your best bet for a little under-the-table foot action. Beware: A pantyhose-clad foot can make suspicious noises when there's a little friction involved.

☙ 13 ❧

SEDUCTIVE STAIRWELL

Risqué Level ●●●

In buildings with elevators, stairwells are good for two things: escape during a fire and quickie sex. Even though you'll be able to hear people in the hallways (and you should keep in mind that they'll be able to hear you, too), stairwell sex feels kind of naughty and public, but the likelihood that someone else will be using the stairwell is fairly low. (Check out the foot traffic for a couple days prior to gauge the likelihood of an interruption). Guys, if you lie down on the incline of the stairs, she'll be able to ride astride you and achieve a different angle of penetration than on a flat bed.

QUICKIE HOT TIP

Ladies, an alternative position is for you to stand on a step slightly above his. This is great for couples who want to do it standing up but have trouble because of their differing heights. (Stairways at home have possibilities, too. See Quickie 32: Stairway to Heaven.)

27

14

AMOROUS OFFICE

Risqué Level ●●●

There's nothing like mixing business with pleasure. Office doors were made with locks for a reason—sex. Nothing can make you feel less like an office drone and more like a living, breathing animal than a midday romp. Paperwork be damned!

"My boyfriend and I work in the same building, and although I have a cubicle, he has an office with a locking door. I always go on an afternoon coffee run, but sometimes instead of getting coffee for a pick-me-up, I surprise him at work, and we do it on his desk. A quickie beats caffeine any day!"

–Catherine, 31

15

GETTING WET

Risqué Level ●○○

Who says your man has to shower alone—or even wants to? Jumping into the shower to give him a quick blow job can be spontaneous and will have him singing happy tunes (all day long!). Guys, just remember that if she fellates you without reciprocation, it's time to repay her once you're out of the shower!

QUICKIE HOT TIP

Share kisses as the shower water splatters on your faces and dribbles between your locked lips. Hold your super-heated, naked bodies close as you let your hands slip and slide over your wet skin, the warm water beating down on you and massaging your necks and scalps.

HALFTIME SHOW

Risqué Level ●○○

If it's impossible to tear your partner away from game-day Sunday or the Monday night kickoff to eat a hot meal together, take TV dinner (and dessert!) to the couch. However, make sure to get it your way, with all attention on you. Quickie sex in front of the TV will probably make him feel like he just won the Heisman Trophy, so dish it up hot and then walk away like nothing happened.

QUICKIE HOT TIP

Don't make a habit of having sex in front of the TV, but as an occasional quickie, it could be a fun score!

BATHTUB BOOTY

Risqué Level ●○○

While she's taking a leisurely soak in the tub, you can surprise her by slipping into the bathroom and getting another kind of leisure. For easier access, you can lift her up to the edge of the tub. While she is perched up there, you'll be doing all the work while enjoying a personal, full-frontal view. This angle will not only be incredibly visually stimulating, but will also give you easy access in fully exploring and stimulating her.

QUICKIE HOT TIP

An inflatable bath pillow—blown up partway—works as a kneepad for the person giving oral sex. Just keep things brief, lest you pop your prop mid-delivery.

~ 18 ~

MORNING DETOUR

Risqué Level ● ○ ○

The most inconvenient—and also the best possible—time for sex is when you're running out the door to get to work. Drop everything, keep your clothes on (except in strategic areas), and get to it. As long as you don't show up at work totally sweaty and disheveled, no one should be the wiser. Just don't make a habit of sneaking into work fifteen minutes late, or people may begin to suspect why your sweater is rumpled and your buttons are askew.

"One of my favorite things about having a quickie just as we're heading out the door is that any anxiety I have about my work-day is forgotten, replaced with fond memories (and lingering scents!) of my morning detour."

–Paul, 33

19

MORNING MAKEOVER

Risqué Level ●○○

Doing make-up is a part of the morning routine for many women. You can add a little spice to the ritual by sneaking up behind her and getting frisky. Bend your love over the sink, placing your hands wherever you want them, and telling her you find her absolutely irresistible before cutting right to the chase. Enter her from behind as you cup her breasts and curl your body around hers, burying your face in her hair. With flushed cheeks and a sparkle in her eye, afterward she won't even need to finish her make-up.

> *I was surprised when my husband snuck up behind me and put the moves on me while I was doing my make-up. The fact that we were in front of the mirror made it even hotter. Watching ourselves bring each other to orgasm was incredibly erotic!*
>
> *–Marisa, 32*

20

TAXICAB CONFESSIONS

Risqué Level ● ● ●

If you're feeling a little frisky and in the mood for a quickie, all you have to do is hail a cab! How's that for fast service? A little backseat naughtiness in a taxi is a great way to heat things up, and it's way more fun than watching the meter run.

QUICKIE ETIQUETTE

Most cabdrivers won't mind too much if you have a quickie in the backseat as long as you don't put them at risk of being pulled over and ticketed for indecent exposure. For a little extra incentive, slip the driver a generous tip at the beginning of the ride to keep his eyes on the road, and not on the rearview mirror. (For a little more privacy en route, check out Quickie 49: Live It Up in the Limo.)

21

COATROOM CANOODLE

Risqué Level ●●●

Volunteer to be the greeters and "coat check couple" at your friend's dinner party. When the party is at its height and you won't be missed, slip into the bedroom where the coats are being kept for some erotic, quick action. The pile of down and leather will help conceal you if anyone pops in.

QUICKIE ETIQUETTE

This quickie needs to be timed just right, sometime in the middle of the evening. Make sure not to neglect your coat-fetching duties, or your secret will be exposed.

22

DINER'S DELIGHT

Risqué Level ●●●

It would take some courage to just throw down and do each other right in the middle of a diner—you never know who the other patrons might be!—but you can dial down the risk by cuddling up in a booth and saving the actual sex for later. A big flowing skirt can go a long way in concealing a lot of below-the-waist activity. Oversized menus, large napkins, and a well-placed winter coat can also help disguise the fact that you're working up an appetite for the real meal once you're alone. Pick an uncrowded time, stick to the back of the restaurant, and don't forget to tip well.

> *I always get really nervous and really excited about doing any-thing naughty in public, but I've found that the right outfit—a loose skirt, an elastic waistband, and no panties—can make the experi-ence that much better. Easy access is the name of the game!"*
>
> –Claire, 27

23

SEXERCISE SCHTUPP

Risqué Level ●●○

Working out is all well and good, but have you made sure to exercise all your muscles today? A little imagination turns that expensive workout equipment into sex furniture. If you keep at those pelvic thrust reps for a while, you'll be able to skip your regular cardio on that stationary bike. Feeling the burn from sex versus bench-pressing will be so much more fun, too, and you'll both be satisfied that you're staying in shape.

QUICKIE HOT TIP

Raising your heart rate—and increasing your breathing and muscle activity before sex—enhances your body's ability to get turned on, acting as a type of foreplay.

24

THE GRASS IS ALWAYS GREENER

Risqué Level ● ○ ○

It's difficult to get motivated to do unpleasant household chores like cleaning the garage or mowing the lawn, but with some sexy incentive, your household duties will be finished in no time. Create a list of tasks for completion, and then reward yourselves with a quickie as you check items off your list.

"Like any red-blooded man, I hate cleaning, but I love sex, so it's less difficult to start cleaning when I know there's a naked reward in the not-so-distant future. Who needs a riding lawn mower when I can get a randy ride from sex?"

–James, 34

25

BEACHCOMBER BOOTY

Risqué Level ● ● ●

Go for a slippery yet sun-soaked quickie. Pick a secluded stretch of beach, the one just outside the lifeguard's range, maybe behind that little outcropping of rocks, to set up camp and get down to business. If you're comfortable, you can even use a little naughty conversation about the eye candy you've been looking at all day to get you started.

QUICKIE HOT TIP

Nothing kills a beach romance like sand in your most tender parts, so make sure you're lying on a blanket and that you've gotten all the sand off your hands before you get started. Make sure to slather on sunscreen as well—getting burned will put a damper on your fire. Keeping baby wipes in your beach bag will be great for a quick cleanup. And if you're not ready for a public encounter, try a secluded or private beach to bring this down to a level two.

51

26

MIDNIGHT SNACK

Risqué Level ●○○

If your partner is a midnight snacker, why not surprise him with a different type of treat? When you hear footsteps in the kitchen, make a beeline there yourself, and have the whipped cream, chocolate sauce, or honey ready for application and licking removal. Bon appétit!

"My husband is always sneaking down to the kitchen for a late-night snack, even though he knows it's unhealthy to eat in the middle of the night. When I hear him get out of bed and creep down the hallway, I follow him and pounce on him in the kitchen. Then I give him something else to snack on—me!"

–Vanessa, 35

27

ELEVATOR "EMERGENCY"

Risqué Level ●●●

A "stuck" elevator is the perfect place for a quickie. Whether you hold the doors open while the elevator is in the basement or pull the emergency switch as it passes between two floors, know that your time is limited. Someone's bound to need that elevator soon, so get to it! Anyone going up?

QUICKIE HOT TIP

It's best to do this stunt in an elevator you're well acquainted with. Nothing spoils a quickie like the fire department showing up to bail you out—naked. Also, beware of security cameras!

28

AQUATIC AROUSAL

Risqué Level ●●●

Water, wet and flowing, is sexual in its very essence. Slip in for a dip; any body of water will do—a pool, a bay, a lake. Drop the bottom part of your bathing suit for a little more action, and you'll both be swooning. This is the most fun—and naughtiest—when accomplished near other people.

QUICKIE HOT TIP

Even though water is wet, it can wash away a woman's natural vaginal lubrication. However, silicone-based lubes stay wet even when you're not. If there's a chance you might engage in erotic aquatic adventures, dab on some lube, and things will slide along with greater ease. Keep in mind that water can also wash away your bathing suit…hold onto it if you don't want to walk out of the water naked!

29

AFTERNOON DELIGHT

Risqué Level ●●○

Mowing the lawn and taking care of the yard make any man all hot and sweaty. If she steps out to water the flowers, watch out: that just might lead to watering her flower. Strip down to nothing in a secluded part of your yard, and get wild in the freshly cut grass.

"There's something about nature—even if it's the well-maintained nature right outside our back door—that just gets me going. Taking my wife right out in our yard just feels primal."

–Andrew, 34

OFFICE MEMO

Risqué Level ●●○

Interrupt a not-so-important meeting with an important message: the urgent need for a quickie. You can write down your missive, perhaps on a sticky note, but keep it simple, something like "I want you now!" For more adventure, try whispering it. Cup your hand around your mouth for added sensuousness and to make sure eavesdroppers can't pick up on your plan.

QUICKIE ETIQUETTE

Make sure you're not interrupting an important call—messing with your paramour's business is a sure way to get the cold shoulder. If you have to wait for the call to finish up, try locking the office door, sitting on the desk, and starting to strip for some foreplay and visual stimulation!

31

KWIKY CAR WASH

Risqué Level ●●○

While supporting a charity car wash might be altruistic, you'll have more fun with your own X-rated one in your driveway. Grab your partner, and get the car and yourselves wet and soapy, making sure you lather his hose extra nicely, while he details your body with his wet tongue. Or lean her up against the car hood and take her from behind, using the water spray from the hose for extra excitement.

QUICKIE HOT TIP

If your driveway isn't exactly private, and you don't want your neighbors to see your slippery fun firsthand, stick to something a little tamer, like a wet T-shirt contest, and then take it inside to finish pimping out the "ride"! (Or for another car wash option, check out Quickie 46: At the Car Wash.)

32

STAIRWAY TO HEAVEN

Risqué Level ●○○

Whether you're on your way up to the bedroom for some sexual fun or heading down to your deck for sun and lemonade, take a brief detour on the stairs for quick satisfaction. Use the stairs to create some creative angles that aren't possible on a flat surface. The landing can give you extra leverage if you need it. The stairs can be great not just for touching those hard-to-reach spots, but also for getting a new perspective on your lover's body as you look at each other from a new vantage point.

> "Fooling around on the stairs really spices things up for my husband and me because it's like having built-in sex furniture in the house. You just need to pay attention to your balance, which can be both challenging and entertaining."
>
> –Leah, 36

33

SUMMERTIME QUENCHER

Risqué Level ●○○

Take time out on a hot summer day to cool down—and heat up—with some ice water by the backyard pool. If you don't want to take a dip just yet, take turns dripping ice water and ice cubes all over each other's bodies—and then licking up the mess. A few strategically placed ice cubes (such as in your mouth!) can really send chills down your lover's spine—or his shaft!

QUICKIE HOT TIP

This also works really well with brightly colored popsicles. Once the colored treats have melted on your lover, trace the sticky trail with your tongue and help clean it all off.

34

QUIET RAPTURE

Risqué Level ●●●

Excuse yourselves during a lull in conversation at a dinner party and slip into the hallway to feel each other up. This quickie is made much hotter by the urgency with which you must act, the need to be silent, and the knowledge that while everyone else is being civilized and talking around the table, you're getting frisky only a few feet away.

QUICKIE ETIQUETTE

This quickie is best accomplished if you make sure you're not hiding in a hallway that is en route to the bathroom or the kitchen. If you get discovered, you can expect this incident to go down in dinner-party gossip history.

～ 35 ～
HEAVY PETTING

Risqué Level ● ○ ○

Sometimes it's fun to recapture those awkward, fumbling, high school moments with a solid sofa make-out session. Instead of jumping right into the nudity and bump-'n'-grind, spend some time groping and caressing each other with your clothes still on. If it helps you get into the spirit, put a movie on in the background (it could be a naughty flick!) and pretend you're watching it.

> *To spice up a couch session and make it a bit more frantic, sometimes my husband and I say things to each other like, 'Hurry up. My parents will be home soon.' Most of the time it just makes us laugh, but it still adds to the fun."*
>
> –Laura, 35

36

THE NAUGHTY HAIRBRUSH

Risqué Level ●○○

Even a well-groomed woman deserves a spanking sometimes. While you're at the sink washing up, your man can slip up behind you, run his hands over your bottom, and grab your hairbrush. If you're the guy trying this and you're not sure how she'll react, be sure to make your moves playful, keep a smile on your face, and maintain eye contact in the mirror.

QUICKIE HOT TIP

If you're into spanking, you can role-play all of the "traditional" disciplinary scenes: teacher and naughty pupil; prison warden and prisoner; or boss and secretary, to name a few. The number and variety of different scenarios is limitless, and having a selection of props and costumes makes the play even more exciting.

37

A SNEAK PREVIEW

Risqué Level ●●●

Liven up the slow parts of a movie and revisit furtive high-school trysts with a little bit of hand action. You might start with a playful yawn-and-stretch move to get your arm around her, and then drop your hand farther down her chest. A braver soul might drop that hand into her lap—*whoops*! As you make your way up her thigh, whisper your dirty thoughts in her ear while keeping one eye on the screen.

QUICKIE ETIQUETTE

Sitting in the back of the theater is a tried-and-true security measure for movie theater nookie, but failing that, a coat over your laps is an excellent way to conceal what you're up to.

38

THE GREAT OUTDOORS

Risqué Level ●●○

The scent of pine and clear mountain air do wonders for awakening the senses, including your erotic ones. Step off the beaten path on your next countryside hike to listen to the sounds of the forest—and each other's soft moans. The further you go off the trail, the more private you'll be...the call of the wild indeed.

QUICKIE HOT TIP

All hikers should be at least a bit knowledgeable about local poisonous plants that make their home along the trail, but when in doubt, remain standing. The only souvenir you should leave the woods with is a hot memory, not poison ivy!

39

CORNER POCKET

Risqué Level ● ● ○

Stealthy sex is almost always the most fun. While shooting pool at the local dive bar, your man can get behind to help you with your technique. This kind of close encounter will rev you up, and waiting in a corner for the next shot is where you can get in some serious action. You probably aren't going to be able to finish your erotic game, but you never know. Those dark, dank corners are definitely good for something.

"Having my boyfriend get behind me and get up close and personal while I'm trying to aim my pool cue doesn't exactly do wonders for my aim and concentration, but feeling his excitement against my legs really gets me going."

–Lauren, 28

40

KING OF THE WORLD

Risqué Level ●●○

Ships ahoy! Boats were made for seafaring lovers. Let the gentle rocking of the boat nudge your bodies closer and closer together as the salty air awakens your senses. String bikinis are made for easy access, but there's something rugged about wearing only a life jacket. Remember, it's not the size of the yacht, but the motion of the ocean!

QUICKIE HOT TIP

A little creativity and knowledge of rigging and knots will have you all tied up and ready for a naughty nautical adventure.

41

TRUCKIN'

Risqué Level ●●○

One of the best places for romance is under the stars! Cruise to a favorite make-out spot, climb into the bed of your pickup truck, and give it your all. With a little planning ahead, you'll have a few blankets to make you a bit more comfortable. But since the idea is to make it fast and furious, a little discomfort won't hurt you; it'll just motivate you to get the job done. The same goes for weather—it'll be more fun in the summer, but plummeting temperatures can inspire you to make your own heat.

QUICKIE HOT TIP

If you don't have a pickup truck, you can try the hood of your car. That will work just as well, but be aware of how much weight you put on the hood without bending it out of shape.

42

A RAVENOUS FEAST

Risqué Level ●○○

Create your own epicurean erotica scene. Keep the wine flowing and, for good measure, throw in some aphrodisiacs such as chocolate and oysters. Skip cleaning up the dishes once in a while and go right to dessert—devouring each other. After a hot meal, keep the warmth flowing and satiate each other right there at the dining room table.

"Sometimes my husband and I tempt each other with scrumptious treats—using our bodies as dinnerware! I mean, who needs a spoon when you have a tongue?"

–Maria, 33

≈ 43 ≈

INTO THE WILD

Risqué Level ●○○

Whether you're in your own backyard or on a true getaway, pitching a tent for two can bring you closer together in more ways than one. Being near the earth, but slightly shielded from it in a tent, feels nice and natural. Get a small enough tent, and you'll be forced to cling to one another—and while you're clinging, you might as well get busy on your erotic adventure. For extra snuggling, squeeze into one sleeping bag, zip off your clothes, and zip up for the night.

> "My girlfriend isn't a big fan of the great outdoors—bugs, wild animals, no TV!—but I can talk her into it once in a while. I just have to make sure that I take good care of her needs while we're out there, like learning how to roast her 'marshmallow' the right way!"
>
> –Kevin, 27

87

44

HOT SEAT

Risqué Level ●○○

Your partner will be happy to have a quiet moment of porch reading interrupted if you let him know what you want. Sit in his lap, and ease your skirt up to your waist—it's a great angle for deep penetration, and you'll get a workout using the arms of the chair as leverage to lift yourself up and down. Guys, this quickie gives you the best seat in the house.

QUICKIE HOT TIP

This is a great position for whispering sweet nothings in your lover's ear—always a great addition to any sexual encounter.

45

FLAMBÉ

Risqué Level ●○○

Ignite your lover's desire with carnal concoctions. Guys, you can throw her up on the counter and ravage her with succulent kisses; or ladies, you can push him up against the stove, grabbing, stroking, or sucking him until he's well done. Serve yourself up on the kitchen table and call it a five-star meal.

"There's something about the heat of cooking that really turns me on. Although I might be craving food when I first start, if my husband comes into the kitchen, it turns into this animalistic hunger that makes me take him right there!"

–Jane, 36

46

AT THE CAR WASH

Risqué Level ●●○

There's nothing like a quickie with a timer! Pull up to the automatic car wash and punch in an order for the longest, most detailed wash you can find. As you slide your car into the bay, slide off your clothes. The darkness and gentle hum of the washers drown out the rest of the world. But once the dryer starts, your adventure needs to end, or others in the parking lot may see more than they bargained for through your shiny clean windows.

QUICKIE HOT TIP

For maximum privacy, choose an automatic car wash without attendants and try to go when the streets are relatively quiet. For a more heart-pounding, stealthy style, hit the wash in broad daylight with a line of cars behind you, letting the rush to the finish boost your adrenaline.

47

I DO...WANT YOU

Risqué Level ● ● ●

There's just something about weddings that brings out a spark in all of us. After the bride and groom declare their undying love, find a secluded spot to declare your passion. A hidden alcove at the reception hall, an unused ballroom, an empty hospitality suite at the hotel, a stand of trees away from the outdoor celebration—the options are endless. If there's a dance, use the power ballads as an excuse to rub up against each other before you scurry off. If you time it right, you can cap off your hurried-up honeymoon with a decadent slice of cake.

QUICKIE ETIQUETTE

Don't be *that couple* at someone else's wedding. This is not the time to play out your public fantasies. Save them for a day when there's no chance of a bride bringing down her wrath upon you, and stick to secluded areas.

48

BOLD ON THE BALCONY

Risqué Level ● ● ●

Give the birds something to chirp about. Sure, there's a king-size bed in the middle of that hotel room, but who wants to mess up the sheets? Slide the balcony door open, and step outside for some quick satisfaction. Not many prying eyes to worry about when you're seven stories in the air, so bare it all and let the wind make you shiver before your partner does.

QUICKIE HOT TIP

If you're in a crowded neighborhood, toss on a fluffy robe. Unless they're behind a pair of binoculars, prying eyes will just think you're enjoying the view. And you are...

49

LIVE IT UP IN THE LIMO

Risqué Level ● ● ○

You may have to shell out some cash, but you'll get a more private space than you would in a cab. That partition will block out the driver, and the tinted windows will block out the world. Better yet, the leather seats give you plenty of room to rip off your clothes and savor the occasion. Spread out and see how much pleasure you can have before the limo pulls to a stop.

QUICKIE HOT TIP

While you can always tell the driver to cruise around, amp up the excitement by giving him a short route. The urgency to get busy before you reach your destination will make the experience even hotter.

50

SEX IN THE STACKS

Risqué Level ●●●

Quiet, bookish types beware—this one requires some gusto. Long reserved for silent reading and research, libraries are the perfect place to indulge in extracurricular activities. Select a secluded area, and reenact your favorite parts of the Kama Sutra. For added ambiance, find the erotica section and read each other a few steamy passages. You never know, you might find some inspiration…

QUICKIE ETIQUETTE

Choose your location wisely here. A larger library will boast a larger number of hidden corners and dusty stacks, and perhaps even some study carrels to balance on as you study anatomy.

51

MILE HIGH MADNESS

Risqué Level ●●●

Sure, joining the traditional mile-high club means heading to the bathroom for a crowded encounter, but why not start the adventure from the comfort of your seat? Spread out a blanket, and let your hands roam free. On overnight flights, the lights will dim, concealing your furtive exploration further. Your partner could even lay in your lap, feigning sleep for any curious passerby. When you just can't take it anymore, rush to the rear of the plane and join the club in a fit of frantic bumping and grinding.

QUICKIE ETIQUETTE

This quickie is best accomplished when you and your partner are in a row by yourselves. To add to the atmosphere, upgrade yourselves to first class and let the bubbly take you away.

52

WORKING UP A SWEAT

Risqué Level ●●○

Running can be an excellent workout, but don't let the end of your jog mean the end of your exertion. With sweat dripping down your bodies and wet shirts clinging, cap off the cardio with a quickie. For a little more adventure, abandon those treadmills for an outdoor run, and flash your partner halfway through to lure him off the jogging trail. You may be too tired to run back home, but your heart rate will be soaring and your satisfaction guaranteed.

QUICKIE HOT TIP
Slide into the shower together afterward for an extension of your exercise, and remember to help each other cool down so you don't pull any important muscles.

Tattoo Chair

NOTES

NOTES

NOTES

ABOUT THE AUTHOR

Audacia Ray is an executive editor of *$pread* magazine, community manager of thePEEQ.com, and author of *Naked on the Internet: Hookups, Downloads, and Cashing In on Internet Sexploration*. She also directed and produced *The Bi Apple*, an award-winning adult film. Audacia lives in Brooklyn, New York. To learn more about her, please visit her website: www.WakingVixen.com.

More Sexy Titles

Available from Sourcebooks

Sex Marks the Spot
69 Racy, Risky, Amazing Places for Intimate Adventure

978-1-4022-1830-9
$12.99 U.S./$15.99 CAN

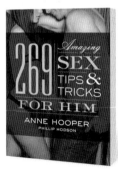

269 Amazing Sex Tips and Tricks for Him
978-1-4022-2453-9
$11.99 U.S./$14.99 CAN

269 Amazing Sex Tips and Tricks for Her
978-1-4022-2454-6
$11.99 U.S./$14.99 CAN

Red Hot Coupons

Available from Sourcebooks

Truth or Dare Sex Coupons
978-1-4022-2665-6
$5.99 U.S./$7.99 CAN

Wild Quickie Sex Coupons
978-1-4022-2666-3
$5.99 U.S./$7.99 CAN

Sexy Coupons for Her
978-1-4022-1029-7
$5.95 U.S./$7.50 CAN

Sexy Coupons for Him
978-1-4022-1028-0
$5.95 U.S./$7.50 CAN

Steamy Coupons
978-1-4022-1091-4
$5.95 U.S./$7.50 CAN

Kama Sutra Coupons
978-1-4022-1030-3
$5.95 U.S./$7.50 CAN